This Recipe Journal belongs to

Recipe for

NAME OF DISH

DATE

INGREDIENTS

SERVES

PREP TIME

TOTAL TIME

PREPARATION

NAME OF DISH

DATE

INGREDIENTS

SERVES

PREP TIME

TOTAL TIME

PREPARATION

Recipe for

NAME OF DISH

DATE

SERVES

PREP TIME

TOTAL TIME

INGREDIENTS

PREPARATION

Recipe for

NAME OF DISH

DATE

SERVES

PREP TIME

TOTAL TIME

INGREDIENTS

PREPARATION

Recipe for

NAME OF DISH

DATE

SERVES

PREP TIME

TOTAL TIME

INGREDIENTS

PREPARATION

NAME OF DISH

DATE

INGREDIENTS

SERVES

PREP TIME

TOTAL TIME

PREPARATION

Recipe for

NAME OF DISH

DATE

SERVES

PREP TIME

TOTAL TIME

INGREDIENTS

PREPARATION

Recipe for

NAME OF DISH

DATE

SERVES

PREP TIME

TOTAL TIME

INGREDIENTS

PREPARATION

Recipe for

NAME OF DISH

DATE

SERVES

PREP TIME

TOTAL TIME

INGREDIENTS

PREPARATION

Recipe for

NAME OF DISH

DATE

SERVES

PREP TIME

TOTAL TIME

INGREDIENTS

PREPARATION

Recipe for

NAME OF DISH

DATE

SERVES

PREP TIME

TOTAL TIME

INGREDIENTS

PREPARATION

Recipe for

NAME OF DISH

DATE

INGREDIENTS

SERVES

PREP TIME

TOTAL TIME

PREPARATION

Recipe for

NAME OF DISH

DATE

SERVES

PREP TIME

TOTAL TIME

INGREDIENTS

PREPARATION

NAME OF DISH

DATE

INGREDIENTS

SERVES

PREP TIME

TOTAL TIME

PREPARATION

Recipe for

NAME OF DISH

DATE

SERVES

PREP TIME

TOTAL TIME

INGREDIENTS

PREPARATION

Recipe for

NAME OF DISH

DATE

INGREDIENTS

SERVES

PREP TIME

TOTAL TIME

PREPARATION

Recipe for

NAME OF DISH

DATE

SERVES

PREP TIME

TOTAL TIME

INGREDIENTS

PREPARATION

NAME OF DISH

DATE

INGREDIENTS

SERVES

PREP TIME

TOTAL TIME

PREPARATION

Recipe for

NAME OF DISH

DATE

INGREDIENTS

SERVES

PREP TIME

TOTAL TIME

PREPARATION

Recipe for

NAME OF DISH

DATE

SERVES

PREP TIME

TOTAL TIME

INGREDIENTS

PREPARATION

Recipe for

NAME OF DISH

DATE

SERVES

PREP TIME

TOTAL TIME

INGREDIENTS

PREPARATION

Recipe for

NAME OF DISH

DATE

INGREDIENTS

SERVES

PREP TIME

TOTAL TIME

PREPARATION

Recipe for

NAME OF DISH

DATE

SERVES

PREP TIME

TOTAL TIME

INGREDIENTS

PREPARATION

Recipe for

NAME OF DISH

DATE

SERVES

PREP TIME

TOTAL TIME

INGREDIENTS

PREPARATION

Recipe for

NAME OF DISH

DATE

SERVES

PREP TIME

TOTAL TIME

INGREDIENTS

PREPARATION

NAME OF DISH

DATE

INGREDIENTS

SERVES

PREP TIME

TOTAL TIME

PREPARATION

Recipe for

NAME OF DISH

DATE

INGREDIENTS

SERVES

PREP TIME

TOTAL TIME

PREPARATION

Recipe for

NAME OF DISH

DATE

INGREDIENTS

SERVES

PREP TIME

TOTAL TIME

PREPARATION

Recipe for

NAME OF DISH

DATE

SERVES

PREP TIME

TOTAL TIME

INGREDIENTS

PREPARATION

Recipe for

NAME OF DISH

DATE

SERVES

PREP TIME

TOTAL TIME

INGREDIENTS

PREPARATION

Recipe for

NAME OF DISH

DATE

SERVES

PREP TIME

TOTAL TIME

INGREDIENTS

PREPARATION

Recipe for

NAME OF DISH

DATE

SERVES

PREP TIME

TOTAL TIME

INGREDIENTS

PREPARATION

Recipe for

NAME OF DISH

DATE

SERVES

PREP TIME

TOTAL TIME

INGREDIENTS

PREPARATION

Recipe for

NAME OF DISH

DATE

SERVES

PREP TIME

TOTAL TIME

INGREDIENTS

PREPARATION

Recipe for

NAME OF DISH

DATE

SERVES

PREP TIME

TOTAL TIME

INGREDIENTS

PREPARATION

Recipe for

NAME OF DISH

DATE

SERVES

PREP TIME

TOTAL TIME

INGREDIENTS

PREPARATION

Recipe for

NAME OF DISH

DATE

SERVES

PREP TIME

TOTAL TIME

INGREDIENTS

PREPARATION

NAME OF DISH

DATE

INGREDIENTS

SERVES

PREP TIME

TOTAL TIME

PREPARATION

Recipe for

NAME OF DISH

DATE

INGREDIENTS

SERVES

PREP TIME

TOTAL TIME

PREPARATION

Recipe for

NAME OF DISH

DATE

SERVES

PREP TIME

TOTAL TIME

INGREDIENTS

PREPARATION

Recipe for

NAME OF DISH

DATE

INGREDIENTS

SERVES

PREP TIME

TOTAL TIME

PREPARATION

Recipe for

NAME OF DISH

DATE

INGREDIENTS

SERVES

PREP TIME

TOTAL TIME

PREPARATION

Recipe for

NAME OF DISH

DATE

INGREDIENTS

SERVES

PREP TIME

TOTAL TIME

PREPARATION

Recipe for

NAME OF DISH

DATE

SERVES

PREP TIME

TOTAL TIME

INGREDIENTS

PREPARATION

Recipe for

NAME OF DISH

DATE

SERVES

PREP TIME

TOTAL TIME

INGREDIENTS

PREPARATION

Recipe for

NAME OF DISH

DATE

INGREDIENTS

SERVES

PREP TIME

TOTAL TIME

PREPARATION

Recipe for

NAME OF DISH

DATE

SERVES

PREP TIME

TOTAL TIME

INGREDIENTS

PREPARATION

NAME OF DISH

DATE

INGREDIENTS

SERVES

PREP TIME

TOTAL TIME

PREPARATION

Recipe for

NAME OF DISH

DATE

SERVES

PREP TIME

TOTAL TIME

INGREDIENTS

PREPARATION

Recipe for

NAME OF DISH

DATE

INGREDIENTS

SERVES

PREP TIME

TOTAL TIME

PREPARATION

Recipe for

NAME OF DISH

DATE

SERVES

PREP TIME

TOTAL TIME

INGREDIENTS

PREPARATION

Recipe for

NAME OF DISH

DATE

INGREDIENTS

SERVES

PREP TIME

TOTAL TIME

PREPARATION

Recipe for

NAME OF DISH

DATE

SERVES

PREP TIME

TOTAL TIME

INGREDIENTS

PREPARATION

NAME OF DISH

DATE

INGREDIENTS

SERVES

PREP TIME

TOTAL TIME

PREPARATION

Recipe for

NAME OF DISH

DATE

SERVES

PREP TIME

TOTAL TIME

INGREDIENTS

PREPARATION

Recipe for

NAME OF DISH

DATE

SERVES

PREP TIME

TOTAL TIME

INGREDIENTS

PREPARATION

Recipe for

NAME OF DISH

DATE

SERVES

PREP TIME

TOTAL TIME

INGREDIENTS

PREPARATION

Recipe for

NAME OF DISH

DATE

SERVES

PREP TIME

TOTAL TIME

INGREDIENTS

PREPARATION

Recipe for

NAME OF DISH

DATE

SERVES

PREP TIME

TOTAL TIME

INGREDIENTS

PREPARATION

NAME OF DISH

DATE

INGREDIENTS

SERVES

PREP TIME

TOTAL TIME

PREPARATION

Recipe for

NAME OF DISH

DATE

SERVES

PREP TIME

TOTAL TIME

INGREDIENTS

PREPARATION

NAME OF DISH

DATE

INGREDIENTS

SERVES

PREP TIME

TOTAL TIME

PREPARATION

Recipe for

NAME OF DISH

DATE

SERVES

PREP TIME

TOTAL TIME

INGREDIENTS

PREPARATION

Recipe for

NAME OF DISH

DATE

INGREDIENTS

SERVES

PREP TIME

TOTAL TIME

PREPARATION

Recipe for

NAME OF DISH

DATE

SERVES

PREP TIME

TOTAL TIME

INGREDIENTS

PREPARATION

Recipe for

NAME OF DISH

DATE

INGREDIENTS

SERVES

PREP TIME

TOTAL TIME

PREPARATION

Recipe for

NAME OF DISH

DATE

SERVES

PREP TIME

TOTAL TIME

INGREDIENTS

PREPARATION

Recipe for

NAME OF DISH

DATE

SERVES

PREP TIME

TOTAL TIME

INGREDIENTS

PREPARATION

Recipe for

NAME OF DISH

DATE

INGREDIENTS

SERVES

PREP TIME

TOTAL TIME

PREPARATION

Recipe for

NAME OF DISH

DATE

INGREDIENTS

SERVES

PREP TIME

TOTAL TIME

PREPARATION

Recipe for

NAME OF DISH

DATE

SERVES

PREP TIME

TOTAL TIME

INGREDIENTS

PREPARATION

Recipe for

NAME OF DISH

DATE

SERVES

PREP TIME

TOTAL TIME

INGREDIENTS

PREPARATION

Recipe for

NAME OF DISH

DATE

SERVES

PREP TIME

TOTAL TIME

INGREDIENTS

PREPARATION

Recipe for

NAME OF DISH

DATE

SERVES

PREP TIME

TOTAL TIME

INGREDIENTS

PREPARATION

Recipe for

NAME OF DISH

DATE

SERVES

PREP TIME

TOTAL TIME

INGREDIENTS

PREPARATION

Recipe for

NAME OF DISH

DATE

INGREDIENTS

SERVES

PREP TIME

TOTAL TIME

PREPARATION

Recipe for

NAME OF DISH

DATE

INGREDIENTS

SERVES

PREP TIME

TOTAL TIME

PREPARATION

Recipe for

NAME OF DISH

DATE

INGREDIENTS

SERVES

PREP TIME

TOTAL TIME

PREPARATION

Recipe for

NAME OF DISH

DATE

SERVES

PREP TIME

TOTAL TIME

INGREDIENTS

PREPARATION

Recipe for

NAME OF DISH

DATE

INGREDIENTS

SERVES

PREP TIME

TOTAL TIME

PREPARATION

Recipe for

NAME OF DISH

DATE

SERVES

PREP TIME

TOTAL TIME

INGREDIENTS

PREPARATION

Recipe for

NAME OF DISH

DATE

SERVES

PREP TIME

TOTAL TIME

INGREDIENTS

PREPARATION

Recipe for

NAME OF DISH

DATE

SERVES

PREP TIME

TOTAL TIME

INGREDIENTS

PREPARATION

Recipe for

NAME OF DISH

DATE

INGREDIENTS

SERVES

PREP TIME

TOTAL TIME

PREPARATION

Recipe for

NAME OF DISH

DATE

SERVES

PREP TIME

TOTAL TIME

INGREDIENTS

PREPARATION

Recipe for

NAME OF DISH

DATE

SERVES

PREP TIME

TOTAL TIME

INGREDIENTS

PREPARATION

Recipe for

NAME OF DISH

DATE

SERVES

PREP TIME

TOTAL TIME

INGREDIENTS

PREPARATION

NAME OF DISH

DATE

INGREDIENTS

SERVES

PREP TIME

TOTAL TIME

PREPARATION

Recipe for

NAME OF DISH

DATE

SERVES

PREP TIME

TOTAL TIME

INGREDIENTS

PREPARATION

Recipe for

NAME OF DISH

DATE

SERVES

PREP TIME

TOTAL TIME

INGREDIENTS

PREPARATION

Recipe for

NAME OF DISH

DATE

SERVES

PREP TIME

TOTAL TIME

INGREDIENTS

PREPARATION

NAME OF DISH

DATE

INGREDIENTS

SERVES

PREP TIME

TOTAL TIME

PREPARATION

Recipe for

NAME OF DISH

DATE

SERVES

PREP TIME

TOTAL TIME

INGREDIENTS

PREPARATION

Recipe for

NAME OF DISH

DATE

INGREDIENTS

SERVES

PREP TIME

TOTAL TIME

PREPARATION

Recipe for

NAME OF DISH

DATE

SERVES

PREP TIME

TOTAL TIME

INGREDIENTS

PREPARATION

Recipe for

NAME OF DISH

DATE

INGREDIENTS

SERVES

PREP TIME

TOTAL TIME

PREPARATION

Recipe for

NAME OF DISH

DATE

SERVES

PREP TIME

TOTAL TIME

INGREDIENTS

PREPARATION

Recipe for

NAME OF DISH

DATE

INGREDIENTS

SERVES

PREP TIME

TOTAL TIME

PREPARATION

Recipe for

NAME OF DISH

DATE

INGREDIENTS

SERVES

PREP TIME

TOTAL TIME

PREPARATION

Recipe for

NAME OF DISH

DATE

SERVES

PREP TIME

TOTAL TIME

INGREDIENTS

PREPARATION

Recipe for

NAME OF DISH

DATE

INGREDIENTS

SERVES

PREP TIME

TOTAL TIME

PREPARATION

Recipe for

NAME OF DISH

DATE

INGREDIENTS

SERVES

PREP TIME

TOTAL TIME

PREPARATION

Recipe for

NAME OF DISH

DATE

INGREDIENTS

SERVES

PREP TIME

TOTAL TIME

PREPARATION

NAME OF DISH

DATE

INGREDIENTS

SERVES

PREP TIME

TOTAL TIME

PREPARATION

Recipe for

NAME OF DISH

DATE

SERVES

PREP TIME

TOTAL TIME

INGREDIENTS

PREPARATION

NAME OF DISH

DATE

INGREDIENTS

SERVES

PREP TIME

TOTAL TIME

PREPARATION

Recipe for

NAME OF DISH

DATE

SERVES

PREP TIME

TOTAL TIME

INGREDIENTS

PREPARATION

Recipe for

NAME OF DISH

DATE

SERVES

PREP TIME

TOTAL TIME

INGREDIENTS

PREPARATION

Recipe for

NAME OF DISH

DATE

INGREDIENTS

SERVES

PREP TIME

TOTAL TIME

PREPARATION

NAME OF DISH

DATE

INGREDIENTS

SERVES

PREP TIME

TOTAL TIME

PREPARATION

Recipe for

NAME OF DISH

DATE

INGREDIENTS

SERVES

PREP TIME

TOTAL TIME

PREPARATION

Recipe for

NAME OF DISH

DATE

SERVES

PREP TIME

TOTAL TIME

INGREDIENTS

PREPARATION

Recipe for

NAME OF DISH

DATE

SERVES

PREP TIME

TOTAL TIME

INGREDIENTS

PREPARATION

Recipe for

NAME OF DISH

DATE

SERVES

PREP TIME

TOTAL TIME

INGREDIENTS

PREPARATION

Recipe for

NAME OF DISH

DATE

SERVES

PREP TIME

TOTAL TIME

INGREDIENTS

PREPARATION

Recipe for

NAME OF DISH

DATE

INGREDIENTS

SERVES

PREP TIME

TOTAL TIME

PREPARATION

Recipe for

NAME OF DISH

DATE

SERVES

PREP TIME

TOTAL TIME

INGREDIENTS

PREPARATION

Recipe for

NAME OF DISH

DATE

SERVES

PREP TIME

TOTAL TIME

INGREDIENTS

PREPARATION

Recipe for

NAME OF DISH

DATE

INGREDIENTS

SERVES

PREP TIME

TOTAL TIME

PREPARATION

Recipe for

NAME OF DISH

DATE

INGREDIENTS

SERVES

PREP TIME

TOTAL TIME

PREPARATION

Recipe for

NAME OF DISH

DATE

SERVES

PREP TIME

TOTAL TIME

INGREDIENTS

PREPARATION

Recipe for

NAME OF DISH

DATE

SERVES

PREP TIME

TOTAL TIME

INGREDIENTS

PREPARATION

Recipe for

NAME OF DISH

DATE

INGREDIENTS

SERVES

PREP TIME

TOTAL TIME

PREPARATION

Recipe for

NAME OF DISH

DATE

SERVES

PREP TIME

TOTAL TIME

INGREDIENTS

PREPARATION

Recipe for

NAME OF DISH

DATE

SERVES

PREP TIME

TOTAL TIME

INGREDIENTS

PREPARATION

Recipe for

NAME OF DISH

DATE

SERVES

PREP TIME

TOTAL TIME

INGREDIENTS

PREPARATION

Recipe for

NAME OF DISH

DATE

INGREDIENTS

SERVES

PREP TIME

TOTAL TIME

PREPARATION

Recipe for

NAME OF DISH

DATE

SERVES

PREP TIME

TOTAL TIME

INGREDIENTS

PREPARATION

Recipe for

NAME OF DISH

DATE

INGREDIENTS

SERVES

PREP TIME

TOTAL TIME

PREPARATION

NAME OF DISH

DATE

INGREDIENTS

SERVES

PREP TIME

TOTAL TIME

PREPARATION

Recipe for

NAME OF DISH

DATE

SERVES

PREP TIME

TOTAL TIME

INGREDIENTS

PREPARATION

Recipe for

NAME OF DISH

DATE

INGREDIENTS

SERVES

PREP TIME

TOTAL TIME

PREPARATION

Recipe for

NAME OF DISH

DATE

SERVES

PREP TIME

TOTAL TIME

INGREDIENTS

PREPARATION

Recipe for

NAME OF DISH

DATE

INGREDIENTS

SERVES

PREP TIME

TOTAL TIME

PREPARATION

Recipe for

NAME OF DISH

DATE

INGREDIENTS

SERVES

PREP TIME

TOTAL TIME

PREPARATION

Recipe for

NAME OF DISH

DATE

SERVES

PREP TIME

TOTAL TIME

INGREDIENTS

PREPARATION

Recipe for

NAME OF DISH

DATE

SERVES

PREP TIME

TOTAL TIME

INGREDIENTS

PREPARATION

Recipe for

NAME OF DISH

DATE

SERVES

PREP TIME

TOTAL TIME

INGREDIENTS

PREPARATION

Recipe for

NAME OF DISH

DATE

INGREDIENTS

SERVES

PREP TIME

TOTAL TIME

PREPARATION

Recipe for

NAME OF DISH

DATE

INGREDIENTS

SERVES

PREP TIME

TOTAL TIME

PREPARATION

Recipe for

NAME OF DISH

DATE

SERVES

PREP TIME

TOTAL TIME

INGREDIENTS

PREPARATION

Recipe for

NAME OF DISH

DATE

SERVES

PREP TIME

TOTAL TIME

INGREDIENTS

PREPARATION

Recipe for

NAME OF DISH

DATE

INGREDIENTS

SERVES

PREP TIME

TOTAL TIME

PREPARATION

Recipe for

NAME OF DISH

DATE

INGREDIENTS

SERVES

PREP TIME

TOTAL TIME

PREPARATION

Recipe for

NAME OF DISH

DATE

SERVES

PREP TIME

TOTAL TIME

INGREDIENTS

PREPARATION

Recipe for

NAME OF DISH

DATE

INGREDIENTS

SERVES

PREP TIME

TOTAL TIME

PREPARATION

Recipe for

NAME OF DISH

DATE

INGREDIENTS

SERVES

PREP TIME

TOTAL TIME

PREPARATION

Recipe for

NAME OF DISH

DATE

SERVES

PREP TIME

TOTAL TIME

INGREDIENTS

PREPARATION

Recipe for

NAME OF DISH

DATE

SERVES

PREP TIME

TOTAL TIME

INGREDIENTS

PREPARATION

Recipe for

NAME OF DISH

DATE

SERVES

PREP TIME

TOTAL TIME

INGREDIENTS

PREPARATION

Recipe for

NAME OF DISH

DATE

INGREDIENTS

SERVES

PREP TIME

TOTAL TIME

PREPARATION

NAME OF DISH

DATE

INGREDIENTS

SERVES

PREP TIME

TOTAL TIME

PREPARATION

Recipe for

NAME OF DISH

DATE

INGREDIENTS

SERVES

PREP TIME

TOTAL TIME

PREPARATION

Recipe for

NAME OF DISH

DATE

SERVES

PREP TIME

TOTAL TIME

INGREDIENTS

PREPARATION

Recipe for

NAME OF DISH

DATE

SERVES

PREP TIME

TOTAL TIME

INGREDIENTS

PREPARATION

Recipe for

NAME OF DISH

DATE

INGREDIENTS

SERVES

PREP TIME

TOTAL TIME

PREPARATION

Recipe for

NAME OF DISH

DATE

INGREDIENTS

SERVES

PREP TIME

TOTAL TIME

PREPARATION

Recipe for

NAME OF DISH

DATE

SERVES

PREP TIME

TOTAL TIME

INGREDIENTS

PREPARATION

Recipe for

NAME OF DISH

DATE

SERVES

PREP TIME

TOTAL TIME

INGREDIENTS

PREPARATION

NAME OF DISH

DATE

INGREDIENTS

SERVES

PREP TIME

TOTAL TIME

PREPARATION

Recipe for

NAME OF DISH

DATE

SERVES

PREP TIME

TOTAL TIME

INGREDIENTS

PREPARATION

www.ingramcontent.com/pod-product-compliance
Lightning Source LLC
LaVergne TN
LVHW081535060526
838200LV00048B/2091